# SECRETS
## OF THE
# ANIMAL WORLD

# FLEAS
## Bloodsucking Parasites

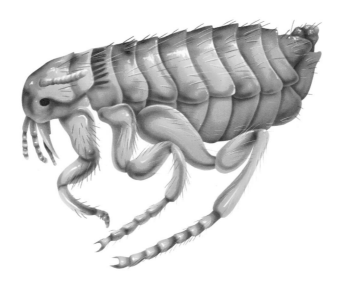

by Andreu Llamas
Illustrated by Gabriel Casadevall and Ali Garousi

Gareth Stevens Publishing
**MILWAUKEE**

**For a free color catalog describing Gareth Stevens' list of high-quality books and multimedia programs, call 1-800-542-2595 (USA) or 1-800-461-9120 (Canada). Gareth Stevens Publishing's Fax: (414) 225-0377. See our catalog, too, on the World Wide Web: http://gsinc.com**

The editor would like to extend special thanks to Jan W. Rafert, Curator of Primates and Small Mammals, Milwaukee County Zoo, Milwaukee, Wisconsin, for his kind and professional help with the information in this book.

**Library of Congress Cataloging-in-Publication Data**

Llamas, Andreu.
  [Pulga. English]
  Fleas : bloodsucking parasites / by Andreu Llamas ; illustrated by Gabriel Casadevall and Ali Garousi.
      p.  cm – (Secrets of the animal world)
  Includes bibliographical references and index.
  Summary: Describes the physical characteristics, habitat, behavior, and life cycle of these tiny, leaping parasites.
  ISBN 0-8368-1650-1 (lib. bdg.)
  1. Fleas–Juvenile literature.  [1. Fleas.]  I. Casadevall, Gabriel, ill.  II. Garousi, Ali, ill.
III. Title.  IV. Series.
QL599.5.L5313  1997
595.77'5–dc21                                                        96-46932

This North American edition first published in 1997 by
**Gareth Stevens Publishing**
1555 North RiverCenter Drive, Suite 201
Milwaukee, Wisconsin  53212  USA

This U.S. edition © 1997 by Gareth Stevens, Inc.  Created with original © 1993 Ediciones Este, S.A., Barcelona, Spain.  Additional end matter © 1997 by Gareth Stevens, Inc.

Series editor: Patricia Lantier-Sampon
Editorial assistants: Diane Laska, Rita Reitci

Printed in the United States of America

1 2 3 4 5 6 7 8 9 01 00 99 98 97

# CONTENTS

# THE FLEA'S WORLD

## Where fleas live

Fourteen hundred species of fleas exist on Earth today. The flea spends its entire life close to its "host," although only adult fleas are actual parasites. Flea larvae are not parasites. Instead, they live on loose particles, or debris, found in the hosts' nests and dens. They also live in human homes.

Fleas can live on many different host animals, such as dogs, foxes, badgers, rabbits, and cats.

About 95 percent of flea species are mammal parasites; the other 5 percent are bird parasites.

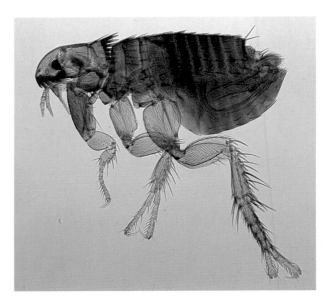

*The flea's body, with its long, leaping legs, is easy to identify.*

*Parasites of all kinds live on our planet, from mountaintops to ocean floors.*

# What is a parasite?

Fleas, bedbugs, and ticks are examples of parasites.

Parasitism is a special association between organisms of two different species. In this relationship, the parasite (usually the smaller animal) alone will benefit. The host does not. This relationship can be so dependent that the parasite is unable to live if it is not in close contact with the host.

A parasitic animal is one that lives off an individual of another species during a part of its life or even during its entire life.

*The forest fly lives on and draws blood from mammals or birds.*

Parasites use their host as a place to find nourishment and shelter.

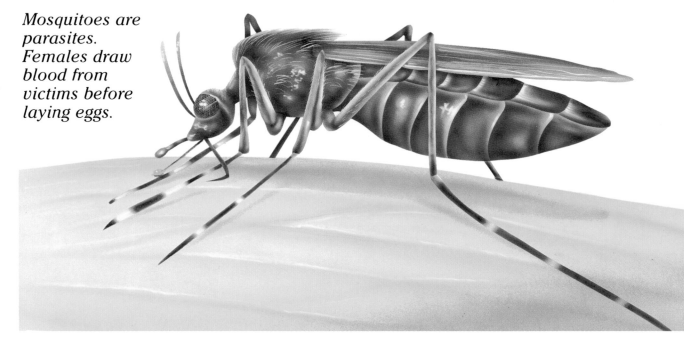

*Mosquitoes are parasites. Females draw blood from victims before laying eggs.*

## Kinds of parasites

The various parasite species do not belong to the same animal group. What characterizes the species is its way of life, not the structure of its body.

Parasite species exist within very different animal groups. These include some protozoans, or single-celled animals; almost all the platyhelminths, or flatworms; many arthropods (especially insects, crustaceans, and arachnids); and numerous annelids, or segmented worms, among others.

Ectoparasites, or external parasites, live on the outside

*Ticks can reach a considerable size. They feed by drawing blood from their host.*

*Many parasites, such as the platyhelminths, look like worms.*

*Of the 40,000 tick species, only a few are parasites.*

*Lice have a stinging-sucking buccal, or mouth, part that they use to draw blood from mammals.*

of the host's body.  Some examples are lice and fleas. Endoparasites, or internal parasites, live inside the cells, between tissues, or in the cavities of the host.  An example is an intestinal worm.

Some parasites prefer to live freely on the exterior if they can find enough nourishment there. These are referred to as facultative parasites.

FLEA

# INSIDE THE FLEA

The flea's body is covered with a chitinous shell that allows it to resist great pressure. It pierces its victims with its buccal, or mouth, parts and draws blood from the victims for nourishment. The flea's body and legs are covered in hard spines and spiny combs that point backward to keep the flea anchored.

**HEAD**
The flea's narrow forehead parts the hairs or feathers of the host so it can move around easily.

**STOMACH**

**CROP**

**BRAIN**

**ANTENNAE**
The flea's antennae contain organs for detecting odors. When the flea rests, its antennae lie in an antennal groove.

**PHARYNX**

**EYES**
The flea's eyes are poorly developed, so its vision is not very good. Some fleas are blind.

**BUCCAL APPARATUS**

**PIERCING STYLET**
The buccal parts form a piercing stylet that points down and back. The stylet is used to pierce the host and draw its blood.

**LABIAL GLAND**

**CLAW**
Each leg ends in two claws, turned outward. The claw's shape depends on the type of feathers or fur the flea's host has.

**EXOSKELETON**
The flea is covered by a protective exoskeleton formed by segments of chitin that overlap like shingles.

**HEART**

**FLAT BODY**
The flea's body is flattened on the sides so it can travel easily through its host's fur or feathers.

**INTESTINE**

**GENITAL APPARATUS**
The last segments of the abdomen form the genital apparatus.

**NERVE CORD**

**HARD SPINES**
The body and legs are covered in hard spines and spiny combs that point backward and help keep the flea from being dislodged by its host.

**OVARY**

**LEAPING LEGS**
The third pair of legs is well adapted for jumping. The flea can leap up to 6 inches (15 cm) high and 12 in. (30 cm) forward.

# LIVING OFF OTHERS

## Adapting and modifying

Parasites are very interested in preserving the lives of the hosts on which they exist. If the host dies, the parasite is left without shelter and easily obtainable food. Then it may also die.

Over time, parasites have adapted, or modified, their bodies. For example, to be able to stick perfectly to the host body, parasites have had to develop special organs called hooks and suckers.

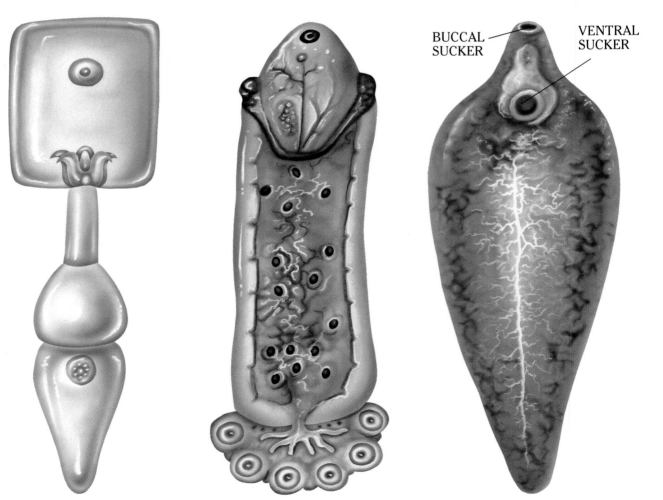

**HOOK SYSTEM OF THE GREGARYNA**

**HOOK SYSTEM AND SUCKERS OF THE MONOGENYDE**

**TREMATODE PLATYHELMINTH**

BUCCAL SUCKER

VENTRAL SUCKER

The parasite's body is simple, since all nonessential organs have been either reduced or eliminated through evolution.

In addition, parasites have well-developed sexual organs. They can lay an incredible number of eggs, sometimes more than sixty million eggs a year!

Each species of parasite has developed its own system for reaching a host. For example, the flea's powerful legs allow it to leap a distance 200 times the length of its own body.

*Parasites stick to their hosts in various ways.*

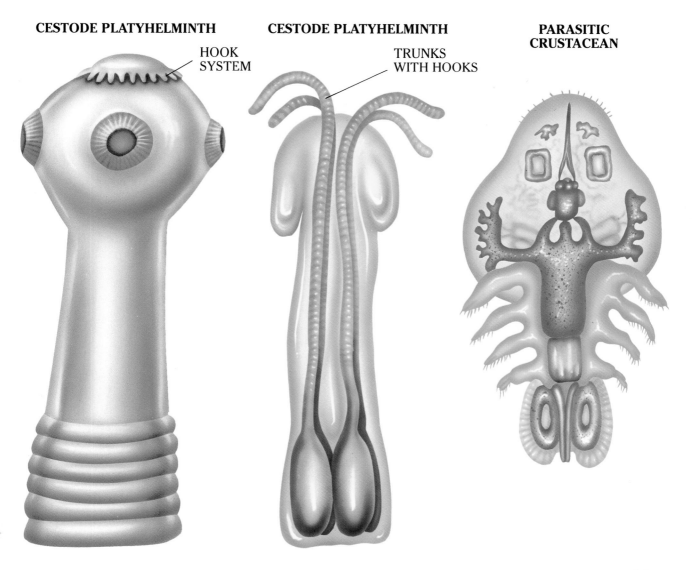

**CESTODE PLATYHELMINTH**

HOOK SYSTEM

**CESTODE PLATYHELMINTH**

TRUNKS WITH HOOKS

**PARASITIC CRUSTACEAN**

## A flea's life

Fleas are not very caring mothers. When females reach maturity, they lay their eggs on the host's body or in the host's nest. The females simply drop the eggs, taking no care about where they fall.

Each female lays several hundred white eggs that usually hatch within the first or second week and turn into larvae. The larvae are white and worm-shaped. They do not have eyes or legs, but they do have strong, biting jaws.

In the species that live in our homes, the larvae prefer dusty crevices, the dirty corners of furniture, or old carpets.

During the two or three weeks of the larval stage, the larvae feed on the decaying organic material they find in dust. Each larva molts twice during this time. When the larva is fully developed, it weaves a cocoon and shuts itself inside. After one or two weeks, the cocoon opens, and an adult flea emerges.

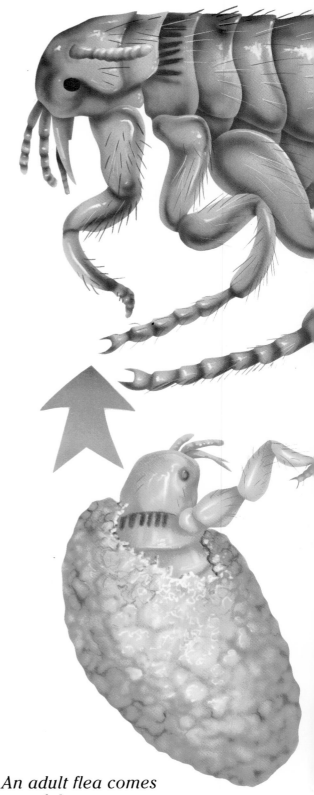

*An adult flea comes out of the cocoon.*

The female flea lays hundreds of eggs.

When an egg hatches, a wormlike larva emerges. It does not have legs or eyes, but it has strong jaws.

The larva weaves a cocoon and shuts itself inside until it transforms into an adult flea.

During the larva phase, the larva molts twice.

# PARASITES AND HOSTS

## Complicated biology

Parasites have complicated life cycles. They often go through several phases during a lifetime. Sometimes they pass through these phases in various hosts.

The tapeworm is a well-known parasite with a complicated life cycle. A tapeworm, also called a solitary, can hide inside a human's small intestine. There, the tapeworm can live up to twenty-five years, taking advantage of the host's food sources. It can grow to 16-20 feet (5-6 m), and some reach 40 feet (12 m).

The segments on the last part of the tapeworm's body are full

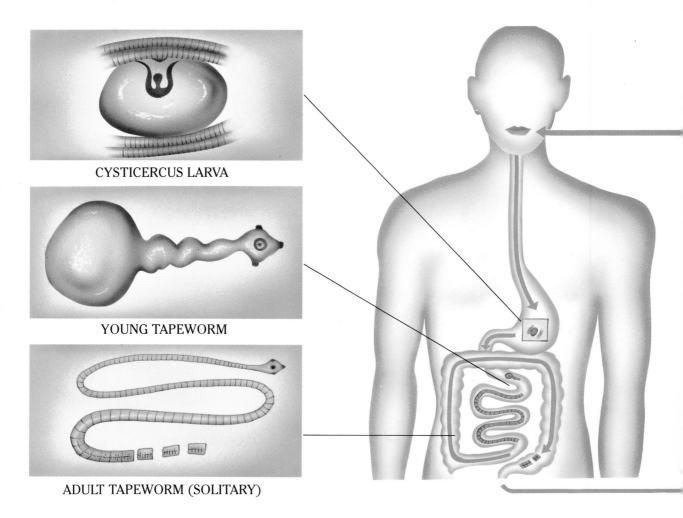

CYSTICERCUS LARVA

YOUNG TAPEWORM

ADULT TAPEWORM (SOLITARY)

of eggs — up to 100,000 in each part. These sections separate from the parasite's body and leave the host's body as waste. This waste can be ingested by a pig. The eggs are then freed in the pig's stomach.

When the eggs reach the small intestine, the eggs hatch, and the embryos (called onchospheres) pass through the intestinal wall.

The onchospheres then migrate through the pig's body and grow until they turn into cysticercus larvae. If humans eat under-cooked, infected pork, the cysticercus uses its hooks to cling to the inside walls of the human's small intestine. In eight to ten weeks, the tapeworm reaches its adult form. Only pork that is well-cooked is safe to eat.

*The presence of a tapeworm in the human intestine can cause diarrhea, a painful sense of hunger, and weight loss.*

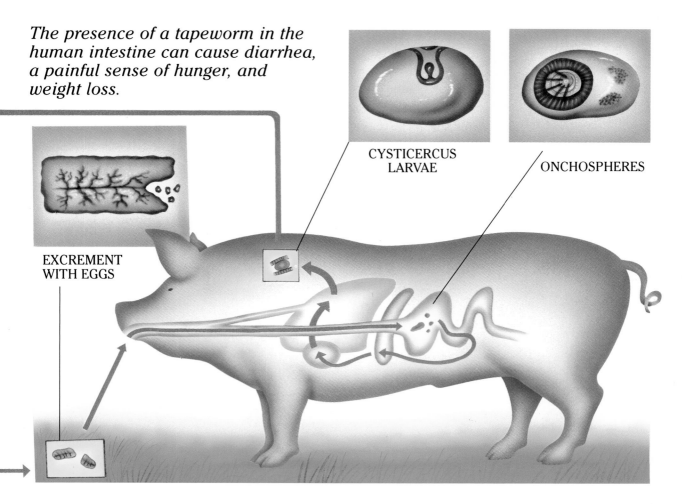

CYSTICERCUS LARVAE

ONCHOSPHERES

EXCREMENT WITH EGGS

## Transmitting diseases

Flea bites can be bothersome and can even provoke allergic reactions and inflammations in humans. But the most serious problem is that fleas transmit diseases. The most dangerous of the infections it can spread is bubonic plague.

Bubonic plague is a disease transmitted by fleas that initially afflicts rats and other rodents. In areas where rats live close to humans, fleas that have lived on infected rats can leap on humans and bite them. In this way, fleas infect humans with diseases that can often be deadly.

*Bubonic plague is a terrible disease transmitted by fleas.*

*Fleas that have been on rats carrying bubonic plague bacteria can transmit this disease to the humans they bite.*

## that fleas detect their victims by heat?

Fleas just out of the cocoon or that have left an old host for some reason are thirsty for blood and on the look-out for a new host. As soon as the flea is near a new host animal, it climbs on this host by taking a huge leap from the ground. To detect the host, the flea identifies the heat of the animal's body. It also feels the air current produced by the host's movements.

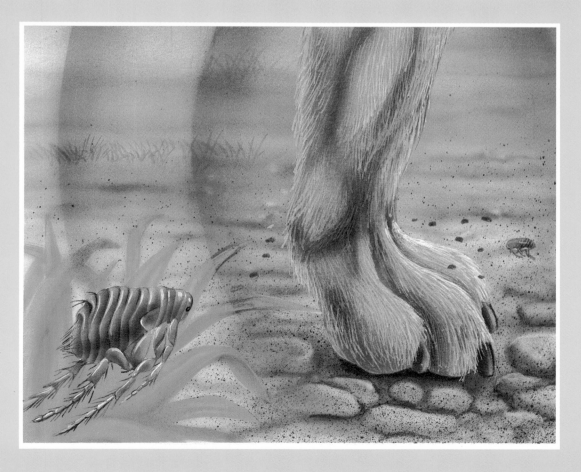

# FLEA ANCESTORS

## The first parasites

Parasitic organisms have existed almost from the beginning of life on Earth. No fossils have remained of the first parasites, however. All of them were very small, and there were no hard parts on their bodies that could easily fossilize.

Parasite life appeared early in the depths of the most primitive oceans. Many of Earth's first inhabitants fell prey to these pesky organisms.

*Early parasites may have looked similar to their descendants — amoebas and flagellates.*

## Primitive fleas

How can tiny flea fossils be preserved for millions of years? A few decades ago, a fossil of a flea that had lived 60 million years ago was discovered. This flea got stuck on a drop of resin from a coniferous tree. The drop of resin completely surrounded the body of the small flea. As the resin hardened, it preserved the tiny corpse.

This hardened resin is called amber. Paleontologists have found many fossils of tiny organisms inside amber.

*The same drop of resin that trapped and killed this flea has preserved its body for millions of years.*

# that flea circuses were popular?

In days gone by, during fairs and other celebrations, people could attend a "flea circus." The audience could observe tiny fleas pulling small carriages or riding a merry-go-round.

When the show was over, the circus owner offered a reward to his fleas by rolling up his shirt sleeve and letting the fleas bite him on the exposed part of his arm so they could draw blood.

# A PARASITE'S LIFE

## Parasite advantages

Scientists think parasites originated millions of years ago from organisms that lived independently of others. So why did they become parasites?

One reason is that there are advantages to life as a parasite. For example, the parasite uses the host's body as a dwelling, so it isn't affected by changing conditions on the outside. In addition, the parasite uses the host as a source of food. It can eat the substances the host ingests, and it can also eat the host's own tissues.

*A parasite can live comfortably even when exterior conditions, such as temperature, are unfavorable.*

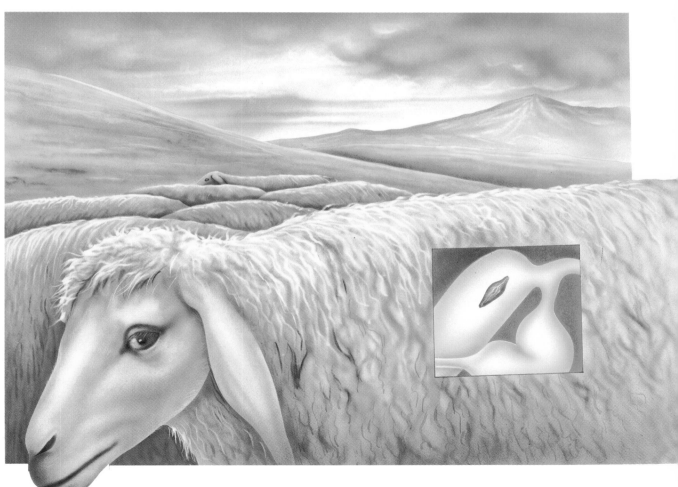

## Did You Know...

### that a flea's bite stings?

A flea bite allows the flea to draw blood, but it also stings the victim. This sting, just as with a mosquito bite, is usually followed by an itchy swelling. When a flea bites, it drops a tiny amount of poison into the wound. This poison irritates the tissue around the bite and causes an inflammation as well as an increase in the amount of blood that flows to the area.

## Where do fleas bite?

Each parasite has its own preference as to where it likes to bite humans.

The flea may crawl underneath a person's body, especially if he or she is lying down, and bite areas covered by clothing.

Fleas usually bite several times in a line along the stomach and back, underneath the waistband of a garment. Nighttime bites that appear on shoulders and thighs can also be caused by fleas. Most leg bites are done by fleas that leap from the floor.

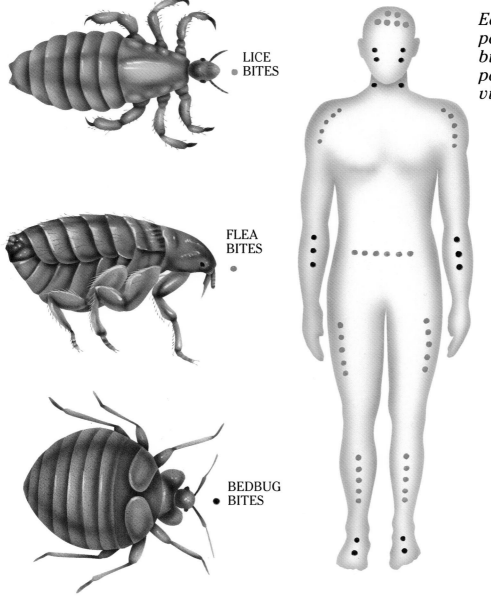

LICE BITES

FLEA BITES

BEDBUG BITES

*Each type of parasite usually bites a certain part of a victim's body.*

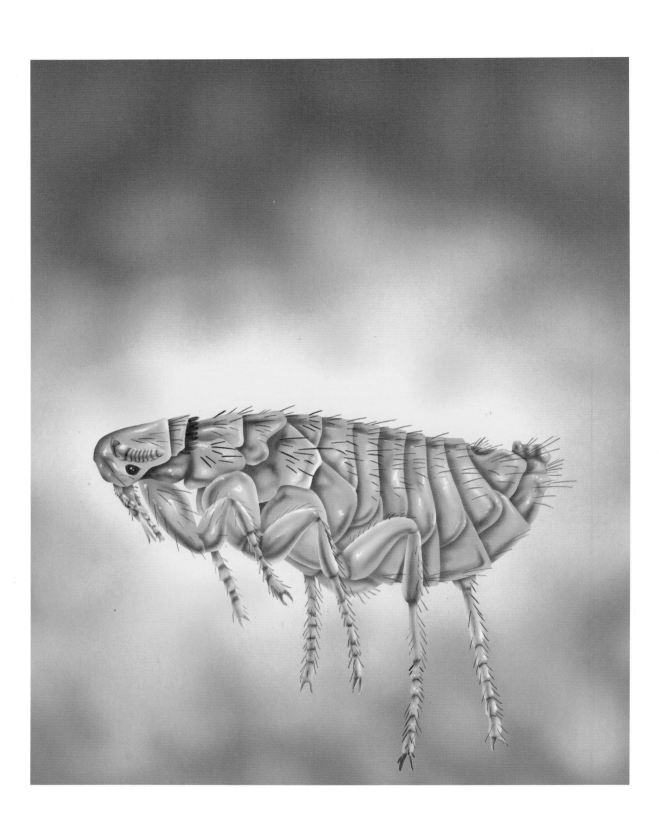

# APPENDIX TO

# FLEAS
## Bloodsucking Parasites

# FLEA SECRETS

**"Superstrong" lice.** Lice have enormous strength in their legs. They can lift more than 2,000 times their own weight. That would be like a human lifting 150 tons!

▼ **Flea leaps.** A flea can leap 6 inches (15 cm) in height and 12 inches (30 cm) in length. To match this, a human would have to jump 330 feet (100 m) in height and 985 feet (300 m) in length.

▼ **Patient fleas.** Fleas can remain inside their cocoons for months if they do not receive exterior stimuli. This is why fleas reappear in abandoned houses when people move back in.

**Cave people with fleas.** Fleas need hosts that live inside permanent nests or dens, so they did not bother humans until they took refuge in caves.

**Prolonged fasts.** Well-fed adult fleas usually live three or four months. But if food is scarce, the flea fasts. If it remains very still, it can live for at least a year.

# APPENDIX TO

# FLEAS
## Bloodsucking Parasites

# FLEA SECRETS

**"Superstrong" lice.** Lice have enormous strength in their legs. They can lift more than 2,000 times their own weight. That would be like a human lifting 150 tons!

**▼ Flea leaps.** A flea can leap 6 inches (15 cm) in height and 12 inches (30 cm) in length. To match this, a human would have to jump 330 feet (100 m) in height and 985 feet (300 m) in length.

**▼ Patient fleas.** Fleas can remain inside their cocoons for months if they do not receive exterior stimuli. This is why fleas reappear in abandoned houses when people move back in.

**Cave people with fleas.** Fleas need hosts that live inside permanent nests or dens, so they did not bother humans until they took refuge in caves.

**Prolonged fasts.** Well-fed adult fleas usually live three or four months. But if food is scarce, the flea fasts. If it remains very still, it can live for at least a year.

**A very powerful poison.**
When a flea bites its host, it drops a small amount of poison into the wound. This drop is approximately a million and a half times smaller than a normal drop of water. The amount of flea poison that actually fits in one drop of water is enough to start itching in as many as two million people.

**▼ Three different hosts.** Some parasites that live in successive animal hosts have complicated life cycles. The small liver fluke passes through a snail, an ant, and a sheep.

1. The number of flea species that currently exist are:
a) about 50,000.
b) about 14,000.
c) about 1,400.

2. Endoparasites are:
a) parasites that live on the exterior part of the host's body.
b) parasites that live in the interior part of the host's body.
c) flea glands.

3. To hold on to their hosts, some parasites use:
a) saliva.
b) formic acid.
c) the back legs.
d) hooks and suckers.

4. The larvae of fleas:
a) do not have legs or jaws, but they do have eyes.
b) do not have jaws.
c) do not have legs or eyes, but they do have very strong jaws.

5. The tapeworm is a parasite that can reach up to:
a) 10 feet (3 m) in length.
b) 40 feet (12 m) in length.
c) 3 feet (1 m) in length.
d) 13 feet (4 m) in length.

6. Amber is:
a) the digestive organ of the flea.
b) drops of hardened resin.
c) the poison that a flea drops into a wound.

The answers to FLEA SECRETS questions are on page 32.

# GLOSSARY

**abdomen:** the section of the body that contains the digestive organs.

**adapt:** to make changes or adjustments in order to survive in a changing environment.

**allergic reaction:** an unpleasant physical reaction to food, pollen, animal fur, or some other substance.

**amber:** a hard, clear, brownish-yellow substance that is hardened resin from a pine tree.

**amoeba:** a tiny, single-celled animal that lives in water.

**ancestors:** predecessors; previous generations of a family.

**annelids:** segmented invertebrate animals, such as earthworms.

**arachnids:** invertebrate animals with segmented bodies and four pairs of legs, such as spiders, scorpions, and ticks.

**bacteria:** tiny single-cell organisms that can cause disease. Some bacteria, however, can also be beneficial.

**biology:** the science of living beings and their life cycles and processes.

**buccal parts:** of, or relating to, the mouth and cheeks.

**chitinous:** made of a rigid substance that forms part of a hard, outer shell.

**cocoon:** the casing that an insect spins around itself and in which it develops into an adult.

**conifers:** trees that bear cones.

**corpse:** a dead body.

**crustaceans:** creatures with an exoskeleton, or shell. Lobsters, shrimp, and crabs are examples of crustaceans.

**current:** a flowing mass of air or water.

**debris:** the scattered remains of something that has been broken or destroyed.

**decade:** a period of ten years.

**den:** the shelter or lair of a wild animal.

**detect:** to notice or discover something.

**eliminate:** to get rid of.

**embryo:** an animal in the very earliest stages of growth, usually in an egg or the mother's uterus, after conception.

**emerge:** to appear or come into plain view.

**exterior:** the outer surface.

**flagellates:** tiny animals, such as protozoans, that have elongated body parts, or filaments, to propel themselves.

**fossils:** the remains of plants or animals from an earlier time that are often found in rock or in Earth's crust.

**hatch:** to break out of an egg.

**host:** the stronger of a pair of organisms in a parasitic relationship; the parasite gets its nourishment and shelter from the host.

**independent:** not controlled by others; capable of living on one's own.

**inflammation:** heat, swelling, and pain caused by an insect bite or another type of irritation.

**ingest:** to eat or swallow something; to take in.

**internal:** located within or inside an object.

**larva:** the wingless, wormlike form of a newly hatched insect; in the life cycle of insects, amphibians, fish, and some other organisms, the stage that comes after the egg but before full development.

**leap:** to jump into the air.

**lice:** tiny insects that live as parasites on humans and other animals. Lice bite their hosts and suck blood.

**mammals:** warm-blooded animals that have backbones. Female mammals produce milk to feed their young.

**modify:** to change something, usually in an attempt to improve it.

**molt:** to shed an outer covering, such as fur or skin.

**paleontologists:** scientists who study life-forms of past geologic periods, usually fossilized bones or tracks preserved in stone.

**parasites:** organisms that live in or on other organisms.

**primitive:** of or relating to an early and usually simple stage of development.

**protozoa:** single-celled organisms that get nourishment by absorbing particles of food.

**reduce:** to make smaller.

**refuge:** a place of safety or protection; shelter.

**resin:** a yellow or brown liquid that oozes from certain trees.

**rodents:** a group of mammals with large front teeth for gnawing.

**species:** animals or plants that are closely related and often similar in behavior and appearance. Members of the same species are able to breed together.

**transform:** to change in form or outward appearance.

**transmit:** to send from one person, place, or object to another.

# ACTIVITIES

◆ One of the most devastating diseases carried by fleas is bubonic plague, often called the black death, which killed about one-third of the European population in the fourteenth century. Do some research about other kinds of diseases carried by fleas that can be passed on to humans and other animals. Other types of insects also carry diseases. What are some of these diseases? In what parts of the world do these diseases occur? What can be done to protect potential victims from becoming infected? Learn some ways pets can be protected from fleas and other annoying and dangerous insects. If your pet gets fleas, how can you get rid of them?

◆ Find a book or article that describes a flea circus. What kinds of tricks did the fleas perform? How do you think the fleas were trained to do their tricks? Or visit a museum or zoo that has an insect exhibit. Compare the size of the flea with other familiar insects, such as beetles, butterflies, and house flies.

# MORE BOOKS TO READ

*ABCs of Bugs and Beasts.*  O. M. Day (Klar-Iden Publishers)
*Amazing Insects.*  (Running Press)
*Bizarre Insects.*  Margaret J. Anderson (Enslow Publishers)
*A Closer Look at the World's Tiny Creatures.*  Jinny Johnson
    (Reader's Digest Association)
*Exploring the World of Insects.*  Adrian Forsyth (Firefly Books)
*Flea's Best Friend.*  Charles Fuge (Gareth Stevens)
*Flying Insects. WINGS* series.  Patricia Lantier-Sampon (Gareth Stevens)
*Little Kit, or the Industrious Flea Circus Girl.*  Karen O'Connor (Dial Books)
*The New Creepy Crawly Collection* (series).  (Gareth Stevens)
*One Hundred Wacky Facts about Bugs and Spiders.*  Brian Hendryx
    (Scholastic)

# VIDEOS

*Feeding Habits of Insects.*  (International Film Bureau)
*The Insect Challenge.*  (Pyramid Film and Video)
*Insect Diversity.*  (Encyclopædia Britannica Educational Corporation)
*Insects.*  (AIMS Media)
*Insects, Insects, Insects.*  (Agency for Instructional Technology)

# PLACES TO VISIT

**Otto Orkin Insect Zoo**
National Museum of
    Natural History
Smithsonian Institution
10 Constitution Avenue
Washington, D.C.  20560

**Australian Museum**
6-8 College Street
Sydney, NSW
Australia 2000

**Canadian Museum of
    Nature**
McLeod and Metcalfe
    Streets
Quebec, Ontario
K1P 6P4

**Royal Ontario Museum**
100 Queens Park
Toronto, Ontario
M5S 2C6

**Auckland Institute and
    Museum**
Auckland Domaine
Auckland, New Zealand

**Cincinnati Zoo Insect
    World**
3400 Vine Street
Cincinnati, OH  45220

# INDEX